"O my luve's like a red, red rose"

In celebration of the world's
admiration of our national
bard, Robert Burns.

Here's to another 250 years!

Contents

GIGLETS PRESENTS...

Tam O'Haggis's
THE
LIFE AND TIMES
OF
ROBERT BURNS

WRITTEN BY FIONA MORTON
ILLUSTRATED BY
TOM BRODIE-BROWNE
AND KAYLEIGH WRIGHT

"A small company with untold potential"

Giglets Ltd
15 Glenbrig
Darvel
East Ayrshire
KA17 0JA
SCOTLAND

First published in paperback in 2009 by Giglets Ltd.

ISBN 978-0-9557297-1-3

10 9 8 7 6 5 4 3 2 1

Printed in Scotland

Author: Fiona Morton
Illustrated by: Tom Brodie-Browne & Kayleigh Wright

Kestrel Press Ltd.
25 Whittle Place
South Newmoor Industrial Estate
Irvine
KA11 4HR
SCOTLAND

Tam O'Haggis

"Opening a Learning Gateway to Scotland"

Today this book is told to you
By a little furry creature.
His name is Tam O'Haggis
And he will be your teacher.

His ginger fur and tartan hat
Make him stand out from the crowd.
He'll tell you all about his home,
Being Scottish makes him proud.

There are poets and inventors,
The list it doesn't end.
So learn it all from Tam O'Haggis,
Your little furry friend!

Prologue

Tam O'Haggis was busy packing for his trip to Alloway to visit Gran and Papa O'Haggis. He put his green tartan cap in his suitcase along with his bucket and spade. Tam hoped to visit Ayr's sandy beaches while he was there.

He looked in the mirror before he left; shaggy, ginger hair was combed, black boots were polished, teeth were pearly white. Tam knew Gran would not be happy if he arrived looking anything less than perfect.

He sat on the train watching the beautiful Ayrshire countryside fly by and looked forward to his summer in Alloway. He could not wait to visit Burns Cottage which lay in the heart of his grandparents' village. Ever since learning about Robert Burns at school, Tam had been desperate to know more about the great Scottish poet's life.

He arrived at the station and was greeted with a great big kiss by Gran O'Haggis. She got bright red lipstick all over his lovely ginger fur! As they walked to Gran and Papa's house he passed Burns Cottage and could not wait for tomorrow when he was going to go inside.

When morning broke, Tam was already awake and after breakfast he ran to the cottage. He opened the door to the home where Robert Burns was born and walked inside...

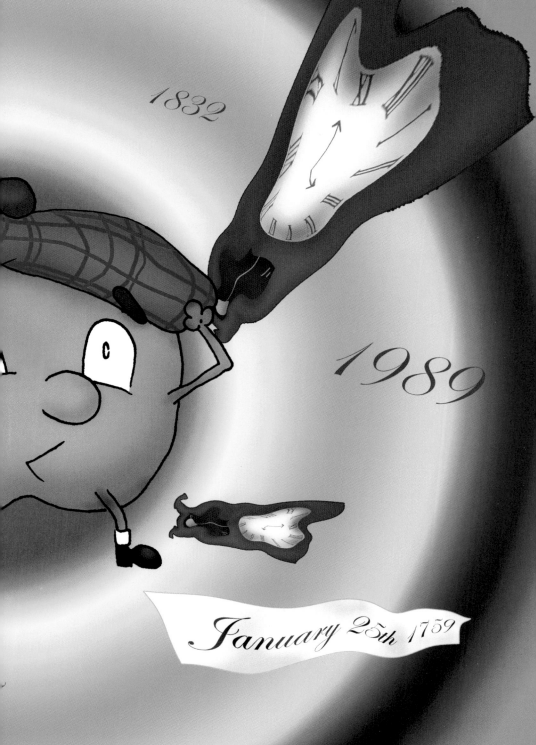

CHAPTER 1

THE BIRTH OF THE BARD
EVENTS FROM 1759-1766

It was like stepping back in time as Tam watched Robert Burns being born in the tiny cottage on 25th January 1759. He was the first son of William and Agnes Burns. Robert was born into a poor and hard working farming family.

Tam could see that Robert did not have a very tasty diet. He also noticed that some of the people chewed on barley for hours to try to fight their hunger.

The rich people tended to have more sugar in their diet, but this led to them having, to Tam's amusement, no teeth!

Tam stood by the fire in the centre of the room and listened intently as Agnes' cousin, Old Betty Davidson, told the children stories about witches and devils.

These stories fuelled Robert's already wild imagination and would inspire many of his creative poems in the future.

Tam was amazed to discover that Robert did not attend school but, instead, John Murdoch was hired by Robert's father and other parents in Alloway to teach their children. John left to go to Dumfries and after that William taught his children instead.

The Burns family was growing rapidly and they moved to a farm called Mount Oliphant. Tam now counted six children in the Burns family; Robert, Gilbert, Annabella, William, John and Isabella.

During harvest time, girls and boys would be paired off to work together. While Tam was busy ploughing the field, Robert had his mind on other matters. He was paired with Nelly Kirkpatrick who would soon become "Handsome Nell" in his song "O, Once I Lov'd a Bonie Lass". He wrote this when he was just 15 years old.

1759 -1766

William and Agnes' very first child

Had an imagination which would run wild.

Instead of helping to plough on the farm,

He would rather have a girl on his arm.

CHAPTER 2

ROBERT'S FIRST STEPS INTO ADULTHOOD
EVENTS FROM 1777-1784

Tam wished they had removal vans back in Burns' time as Robert's family were set to move farm again, this time to Lochlie, a farm on the outskirts of Tarbolton.

During his teenage years, Robert and his brothers and sisters attended dance classes in Tarbolton. Tam tried to join in, but slipped on the wooden floor and landed in a heap in the corner.

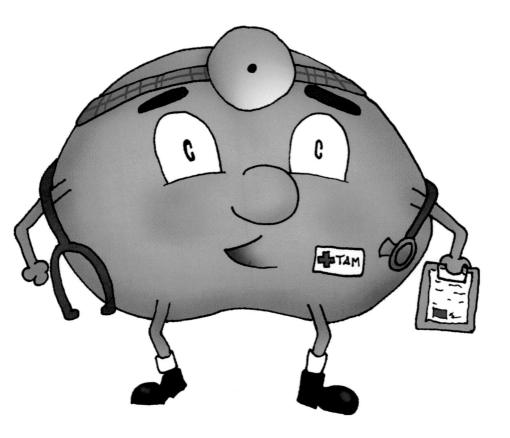

Watching Robert grow up made Tam very grateful for all the benefits of the 21st century which he had previously taken for granted. The improvements in medicines were what struck Tam the most.

There were few medicines available to Robert in his lifetime and home treatments were usually used instead. Robert would see many of his friends and family die at a young age from diseases which are now easily cured.

Tam also saw that poor children often wore the same clothes for months at a time. Poverty led to people only being able to wash their faces on a Sunday.

Tam could only imagine what his gran would say if he only washed once a week. How grubby his fur would be!

In the winter of 1780, Burns became the first president of the Bachelors' Club. They met every fourth Monday and elected a new president at every meeting. In July 1781, Robert was inducted as a Freemason and later became Depute Master of the Lodge.

Tam chased after the Burns family's horse and cart as they moved house again after the death of Robert's father. They rented Mossgiel, a farm near Mauchline, in Ayrshire.

When Tam followed Robert out into the field, he noticed that farming in Robert's time was very different from what he was used to seeing. He looked around but could not see any tractors, which he thought was strange.

Across the field he could see men and horses guiding something wooden around. Tam realised that this must have been how they ploughed the

Later that day, Robert was ploughing when he overturned a fieldmouse's nest. Robert was inspired to write the poem "To a Mouse" after his field-hand, John Lambie, began chasing after the little creature "wi' murdering pattle". In this poem he showed his talent to see everything and everyone as equal.

"I'm truly sorry man's dominion
Has broken Nature's social union,
An' justifies that ill opinion
  Which makes thee startle
At me, thy poor, earth-born companion
  An' fellow mortal!"

Robert was often inspired to write about events in his life. Tam followed Robert to church one Sunday where they watched a louse crawl over a lady's bonnet. This was where Robert got his idea to write his poem "To a Louse".

"Ye ugly, creepin, blastit wonner,
Detested, shunn'd by saunt an' sinner,
How daur ye set your fit upon her-
Sae fine a lady!
Gae somewhere else and seek your dinner
On some poor body."

1777 - 1784

Robert's family continued to move,
In Tarbolton hall they found their groove.
Burns wrote about a wee fieldmouse,
A lamb, two dogs and even a louse.

CHAPTER 3

THE FIRST LOVES OF
ROBERT BURNS
EVENTS IN 1785

Robert, now 25 years old, started courting Elizabeth Paton. During this time, Elizabeth became pregnant and gave birth to Robert's first child, Elizabeth Burns.

Tam followed Robert and Elizabeth to Tarbolton Church where they had to ask for forgiveness after having a child without being married. Elizabeth Burns was handed over to Robert's mother to raise as her own.

Later the same year, Robert began dating Jean Armour and she too became pregnant. When Robert discovered this he wrote her a letter promising to marry her.

Robert was made to ask for forgiveness again for having another child outside of marriage, as the church did not approve of his actions.

It was at this time, Tam discovered that most people were strongly influenced by the Bible and would lead their lives how the church taught them.

Jean's parents were not fond of Robert and when they found out their daughter was going to have a child with him, they decided to send Jean away to live with her aunt in Paisley. Tam felt sad about this as it seemed that Robert was being torn apart from his true love.

"Miss Millar is fine, Miss Markland's divine,
Miss Smith she has wit, and Miss Betty is braw,
There's beauty and fortune to get wi' Miss
Morton;
But Armour's the jewel for me o' them a'."

Tam was surprised with Robert's ability to put Jean to the back of his mind and attract more ladies. He was a handsome man and full of charm.

Once Jean had left, he began courting Margaret "Highland Mary" Campbell. They planned to move to Jamaica together and she returned home to Argyll so she could prepare for their journey.

Robert had to delay these plans and before they could meet again Mary died in Greenock.

1785

Robert's first love was Elizabeth Paton,

She had a child while they were just dating.

Next there was Jean, who fell pregnant too,

He planned for Jamaica but this soon

fell through.

CHAPTER 4

BURNS FOR THE PEOPLE
EVENTS FROM 1786-1787

Tam was excited when Robert sent his poems away to John Wilson, a Kilmarnock printer, with the hope of them being published.

In the summer of 1786, Robert's dream came true as "Poems Chiefly in the Scottish Dialect" had 612 copies printed. This book included "To a Mouse" and "The Holy Fair".

Many of the poems included in the Kilmarnock Edition, as it is also called, were written at Mossgiel Farm.

Tam was so happy to see Robert's hard work finally pay off.

In November, Tam travelled with Robert to Scotland's capital city, Edinburgh, where Robert hoped to make a name for himself. He met many important people during his visit to Edinburgh.

Tam found a top hat and decided to swap his old tartan bonnet for it to try to smarten himself up in front of these new people.

Robert made some good friends when he was in Edinburgh, including Frances Anna Dunlop who he wrote to for the rest of his life.

James Johnson, a publisher, asked Robert to help him edit a collection of Scottish folk songs called "Scots Musical Museum".

There were five volumes of this book published over 16 years and Robert supplied over 150 songs to the collection, including "Auld Lang Syne".

Tam was interested to find this out, as "Auld Lang Syne" was one of his favourite Burns poems. He learned it was actually written to go along with an already composed tune and is now sung all over the world to celebrate New Year.

"Should auld acquaintance be forgot,
And never brought to mind?
Should auld acquaintance be forgot,
And days o' auld lang syne?"

1786-1787

As Robert's career began to shine,

He wrote the classic, "Auld Lang Syne".

To Edinburgh he went during the winter,

To find another willing printer.

CHAPTER 5

RETURN TO MAUCHLINE
EVENTS FROM 1787-1788

Robert Burns, now a successful poet, made his way back to Mauchline. Tam looked on fondly as Jean's parents decided that he was acceptable for their daughter and welcomed him warmly.

At a Christmas tea party, Tam noticed Robert turn his attention to yet another pretty girl, Nancy McLehose. The pair had planned to meet again, but Robert fell from a horse and cart and badly hurt his knee.

Tam tried to jump down to see if Robert was alright, but this was too high for the little haggis to jump from. Worried, he sat on the edge of the carriage as people around helped Robert back to his feet.

Robert and Nancy continued their relationship through a series of loving letters, where they used the secret names of 'Sylvander' and 'Clarinda'.

Robert and Nancy were never able to publicly announce their love, as Nancy was already married. After meeting again, they decided it would be best to end their relationship.

Tam was pleased this happened as he thought Robert should really be with his true love, Jean.

Robert wrote 'Ae Fond Kiss', a tragic love poem for Nancy, describing his broken heart after the love that could never be.

"Had we never lov'd sae kindly,
Had we never lov'd sae blindly,
Never met-or never parted-
We had ne'er been broken-hearted."

When Jean fell pregnant for the second time, Robert was no longer looked on fondly by her parents.

On a lovely spring day in 1788, Tam took off his bonnet and combed his hair before going to watch as Robert and Jean were finally married in a private ceremony in Mauchline.

1787-1788

On return to Mauchline his welcome was warm,

But between Jean and Nancy his heart was torn.

Though Robert had much admired young Nancy,

He married Jean Armour, his only true fancy.

CHAPTER 6

LIFE ON ELLISLAND FARM
EVENTS IN 1789

Robert decided to rent Ellisland, a farm in Dumfries. There was no farmhouse there when he bought it, so he employed a local builder to build one.

Tam was very tired from all the travelling while following Robert back and forth between Ellisland and Mauchline, as Jean still lived in her home town.

As Tam sat down, he was relieved to see Robert and Jean finally move in to Ellisland Farm. It was here that Robert wrote "Tam O'Shanter" which was originally written to go with a drawing of Kirk Alloway in a book of Scottish antiques.

Tam loved the story of Tam O'Shanter. His favourite part was when Tam O'Shanter and Meg were being chased to the bridge by the witches.

In September 1789, Robert began work as an exciseman, which involved travelling on horseback between towns, collecting people's taxes.

Tam felt sorry for Robert as he could see that Robert did not like his job as he did not want to take money from poor people. It was from these feelings he wrote the poem 'The Deil's Awa Wi' Th' Exciseman '.

"The Deil cam fiddling thro' the town,
And danc'd awa wi' th' Exciseman,
And ilka wife cries:-'Auld Mahoun,
I wish you luck o' the prize, man!'"

Tam was upset to see that Robert was becoming ill over the winter of 1789, as he was overworked from his excise duties and from running the farm at Ellisland. He continued to write more great poems even when he was ill including "Willie Brew'd a Peck o' Maut".

"We are nae fu', we're nae that fu'
But just a drappie in oor e'e
The cock may craw, the day may daw
But aye we'll taste the barley bree."

1789

With his new bride Robert moved to a farm,
His kids in tow and a newborn in arm.
He began a new job as a taxman in autumn,
Yet nothing but tiredness and illness it
brought him.

CHAPTER 7

NEW ARRIVALS IN DUMFRIES
EVENTS FROM 1790-1794

Tam couldn't believe that Robert had yet another child outside of marriage, this time to Helen Anne Park. They had formed a relationship over the time that Robert had spent at her uncle's inn.

He had been forced to stay here after his excise duties, when bad weather stopped him from returning home.

Tam hid under a bed as he was scared of the thunder and lightning.

The child was named Elizabeth Burns and Robert's wife brought her up as her own daughter. Jean had just given birth to another child herself, William Nicol Burns. Tam counted that this was Robert's ninth child.

The Burns family had to move from Ellisland when their rent was ended. Over his three years at Ellisland, Tam calculated that Robert had written over 130 songs there.

It was the beautiful, peaceful countryside around the farm which had inspired Robert to write many of his famous poems about nature, since he loved the great outdoors.

The family moved to a three roomed house in Dumfries and Jean gave birth to another child, Elizabeth Riddel Burns.

With the family continuing to increase, they moved again to a bigger house in Dumfries.

Tam had now given up counting how many homes the Burns family had lived in and wondered if they might be better to buy a caravan!

1790-1794

Robert had a child with an innkeeper's niece,

Not long after this he moved to Dumfries.

The family moved to a new house again,

After Elizabeth, child number ten.

CHAPTER 8

ROBERT'S FINAL YEARS
EVENTS FROM 1794-1796

During the cold winter, Tam rode along with Robert as he completed his excise duties. At this time, Robert's health took a turn for the worse, due to the long hours and poor weather he worked through.

His ill health reached a peak when he suffered from a short spell of rheumatic fever.

Despite his ill health, he still managed to continue his writing. Tam agreed with Robert's views on fairness between all humans.

Robert's poem "Is There For Honest Poverty" was written because of a war in France where people wanted to be treated equally.

"For a' that, an' a' that,
Their tinsel show, an' a' that,
The honest man, tho' e'er sae poor,
Is king o' men for a' that."

Tam was worried as he watched Robert's health continue to deteriorate. Robert's friend, Doctor Robert Maxwell, recommended that he should go to the Solway Coast for two weeks of swimming in the sea. This only led to Robert becoming more unwell.

Tam was not surprised that the swimming did not improve Robert's health, as he put one foot in the water and thought he had turned to ice! He decided to find a warm place to wait for Robert until he had finished his treatment.

As Tam travelled back to Dumfries, he could see Robert was not getting any better and all his years of hard work were finally beginning to take their toll on his health.

Tam watched Jean help Robert into the bed where he would spend his last days. Robert Burns was only 37 years old and Tam could not believe this was a normal lifespan for people of Robert's background.

On 21st July 1796 Tam stood by the poet's bed as Robert Burns took his final breath, only three days after returning home from his trip to the Solway Coast.

There were many things Tam knew that led to Robert's death; his poor diet, lack of healthcare, the long hours working on the farm and as an exciseman, as well as the cold nights he would stay up late and write his famous poems by candlelight.

Tam wondered how things would be without his works.

Jean was pregnant when Robert died and she gave birth to Robert's twelfth child, Maxwell Burns, on the day of Robert's funeral, the 25th July.

1794 - 1796

Through his ill health he continued along,

He managed to pen another great song.

To the coast to improve his health he would go,

But died a great Scot, who all men would

know!

Epilogue

Tam opened the door, leaving Robert's family in Dumfries. He walked out of the cottage into the bright sunlight. He was back in Alloway again; the town where his favourite poet had begun his life 250 years ago.

Tam finally appreciated the hard work and dedication that Robert Burns had put into all of his works. His life had been very difficult and riddled with poverty and ill-health but he had struggled through this to become one of Scotland's greatest icons.

Robert had been born to a poor farming family and although he is now a world famous poet, he never earned enough money during his lifetime to get himself out of poverty. He struggled on as both a farmer and an exciseman as well as a loving father to all his children.

Tam thought that if Burns had been born during this century then he would have been a multi-millionaire. It had been a long day for Tam following Robert around, but he had learned so much about the life and times of the great Scottish poet.

Everyone has their favourite Burns poem, whether it is the tale of Tam O'Shanter's terrifying horse ride home or the human kindness shown in "To a Mouse". For Tam it was "Auld Lang Syne", as it always brought his family together with their arms linked on Hogmanay.

Tam would never forget the day he had spent following Robert Burns' life. It was 250 years since the birth of the poet but his songs and poems are still as alive today as they were back then. Tam knew that Scotland's culture and heritage had benefited so much from the work of the great Scottish poet.

The Life and Times of Robert Burns
The Poem

William and Agnes' very first child
Had an imagination which would run wild.
Instead of helping to plough on the farm,
He would rather have a girl on his arm.

Robert's family continued to move,
In Tarbolton hall they found their groove.
Burns wrote about a wee fieldmouse,
A lamb, two dogs and even a louse.

Robert's first love was Elizabeth Paton,
She had a child while they were just dating.
Next there was Jean, who fell pregnant too,
He planned for Jamaica but this soon fell through.

As Robert's career began to shine,
He wrote the classic, "Auld Lang Syne".
To Edinburgh he went during the winter,
To find another willing printer.

On return to Mauchline his welcome was warm,
But between Jean and Nancy his heart was torn.
Though Robert had much admired young Nancy,
He married Jean Armour, his only true fancy.

With his new bride Robert moved to a farm,
His kids in tow and a newborn in arm.
He began a new job as a taxman in autumn,
Yet nothing but tiredness and illness it brought him.

Robert had a child with an innkeeper's niece,
Not long after this he moved to Dumfries.
The family moved to a new house again,
After Elizabeth, child number ten.

Through his ill health he continued along,
He managed to pen another great song.
To the coast to improve his health he would go,
But died a great Scot, who all men would know!

Places of Interest

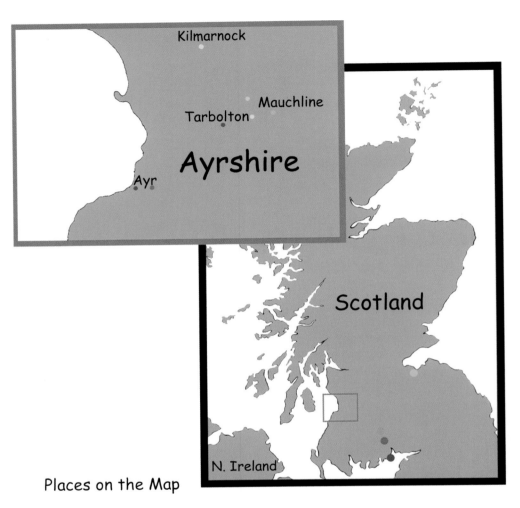

Places on the Map

- Alloway – birthplace of Robert Burns
- Mount Oliphant – farm near Ayr where the Burns family moved in 1766
- Lochlie – farm near Tarbolton where the Burns family moved in 1777
- Tarbolton – town where Robert attended dance classes
- Mossgiel – farm near Mauchline where Burns family moved in 1784
- Mauchline – town where Robert and Jean got married
- Kilmarnock – where the famous Kilmarnock Edition was first printed
- Edinburgh – the capital of Scotland, where Robert went to be famous
- Ellisland – farm near Dumfries where Robert, Jean and their children moved in 1789
- Dumfries – town in south Scotland where Robert lived his final years
- Solway Coast – Robert swam in the sea here to try to get better

Timeline

25th Jan 1759 – Birth of Robert Burns
1765 – John Murdoch hired to teach children
1766 – Burns family move to Mount Oliphant
1774 – Robert writes first poem
1777 – Burns family move to Lochlie
11th Nov 1780 – Robert and friends start the Bachelors' Club
4th July 1781 – Robert becomes a Freemason
13th Feb 1784 – Robert's dad dies
1784 – Burns family move to Mossgiel
22nd May 1785 – Birth of Elizabeth Burns, Robert's first child
July 1785 – Robert becomes Master of the Lodge
1785 – Robert writes "To a Mouse"
1786 – Robert writes "To a Louse"
31st July 1786 – The Kilmarnock Edition is printed
3rd Sept 1786 – Birth of twins, Robert and Jean Burns
1787 – The Edinburgh Edition is printed
Dec 1787 – Robert dates Nancy McLehose
1788 – Birth of son by Nancy's servant
1788 – Jean gives birth to twin girls
2nd May 1788 – Robert and Jean are married
June 1789 – Robert and Jean move into Ellisland
18th Aug 1789 – Birth of Frances Robert Burns
1st Sept 1789 – Robert begins work as an exciseman
31st Mar 1790 – Helen Anne Park gives birth to Elizabeth Burns
9th Apr 1790 – Jean gives birth to William Nicol Burns
10th Sept 1791 – Burns family move to house in Dumfries
21st Jan 1792 – Jean gives birth to Elizabeth Riddel Burns
12th Aug 1794 – Jean gives birth to James Glencairn Burns
Winter 1794 – Robert begins to fall ill
1795 – Robert writes "Is There for Honest Poverty"
3rd-16th July 1796 – Robert goes to Solway Coast
18th July 1796 – Robert returns to Dumfries
21st July 1796 – Robert Burns dies aged 37
25th July 1796 – Robert is buried in Dumfries and Jean gives
                        birth to Maxwell Burns

Glossary

Chapter 1

Barley - a tall grass-like plant whose seeds are used for food

Rapidly - quickly

Ploughing (to plough) - turning over soil with a plough

Chapter 2

Poverty - living without much money

Freemason - a member of an international male group which gives money to charities and has secret rules and signs

Depute Master of the Lodge - someone who helps to lead his lodge. They often have many years of experience so they can guide their lodge as best as possible

Bachelors' Club - a group set up by Robert, Gilbert, and five friends. The aim of the club was to allow the men to forget about the hard work they had to do and to make great friends

Field-hand - helper on the farm

Louse - a small grey creature that likes to live in damp places

Chapter 3

Courting (to court) - dating

Approve - to allow

Influence - power

Chapter 4

Published - made into a book

Chapter 6

Employed - to hire to work

Kirk Alloway - a church in Alloway

Chapter 8

Rheumatic fever - a disease which affects the joints in the body and can damage the heart

Lifespan - lifetime

Healthcare - treatment for diseases

Epilogue

Hogmanay - New Year's Eve

"A small company with untold potential"

Giglets is a group of friends,
With enterprising hopes.
It comprises two young ladies,
And four business-minded blokes.

Craig Johnstone - Managing Director
Gavin Curr - Finance Director
Scott Francis - Sales Director
Tom Brodie-Browne - Art and Design Director
Kayleigh Wright - Designer
Fiona Morton - Lead Author

We would like to thank all of our readers and those people who have believed in our ambitious endeavours.

Giglets Ltd
15 Glenbrig
Darvel
Ayrshire
KA17 0JA

Tel : 07957242339
Email : giglets.limited@giglets.co.uk
Website : www.giglets.co.uk